The first steps in understanding any child with autism is to accept them, appreciate them and love them for who they are.

Uniquely Made

A Very Candid Look at How My Two Autistic Sons Made Me a Better Parent

A novel by

Freeman L. Semons, Jr.

MORNING BREEZE PUBLICATIONS

Uniquely Made

ISBN: 978-1542577366

Morning Breeze Publications
Email: morningbreezepub@gmail.com

First Morning Breeze Publications paperback printing: April 2017

Printed in the United States of America.

Book cover design and layout by Freeman L. Semons, Jr.

Table of Contents

Acknowledgements

To God Almighty, for blessing me
with the art of storytelling

To my late mother Essie R. Semons,
for always believing in me

To my father Freeman Semons, Sr.,
for your wisdom and guidance

To Wanda Bolden, Steve Thomas, Melissa Andrashie, Pamela Bolden, Kenneth Brumfield & Brian Davis, for your endless words of encouragement, inspiration and support

To my sisters, my brother and my cousin (Donna Semons-Pipkins, Karen Semons-Thomas, Crystal Dirden, Mary Norton, James Semons & Regina Brown), for always being there no matter the time, day or season

To my children (Khaila, Elijah & Emmanuel), for your unconditional love, encouragement, appreciation and support

A very special thank you to every Special Ed educator Elijah and Emmanuel have been blessed to have throughout their academic journeys for lessons taught and lessons learned.

Uniquely Made: An Introduction

I have a confession to make. This book almost didn't get written. I say almost because even though the idea of writing a book about my autistic sons had been floating around in my thoughts for quite some time, I really didn't have a clear, definitive way of going about it. All of that changed after I had some very in-depth conversations with my sister Donna, my daughter Khaila, my cousin Regina and my good friend Melissa on the subject of my enduring role as a dedicated, loving parent to my children and of the way I continue to place their needs, the boys in particular, above my own. Long story short, all four of them felt—agreed—that the best person qualified to tell Elijah and Emmanuel's unique story in a way that would present them as two regular kids who didn't view themselves as being different from anyone else is the one person who knows them best. I came to agree with everything the four of them had to say on the subject of my sons and so here we are.

Uniquely Made is a story about the challenges, trials, struggles, changes, advocacies, heartbreaks, tears, duties, responsibilities, setbacks and sacrifices that come with being a single parent and caregiver of two autistic sons. It can also be viewed as an uplifting, encouraging, insightful and enduring account of two uniquely made boys who are true blessings in every sense of the word. Whether you are a parent raising a special needs child with a spouse or significant other, raising them alone or know of someone who has a special needs child of their own, this book is meant for you. With all of the many challenges and difficulties that comes from raising special needs children in today's ever-changing society, it can become very easy to lose yourself in overwhelming nature of your parental duties to the point where you feel like your daily efforts aren't making any change, breakthrough or difference in the life of your child, but I am here to tell you your efforts do matter greatly to them (even if they can't always find the right way to say or share it) and continues to make a very significant difference in ways that aren't always visible at first glance. I know of this firsthand because I speak from years of parental experience on the subject and it has made me a better parent, a better person, as a result.

In closing, I would like to thank you, the reader, for purchasing this book with the hope that it will serve as a constant source of inspiration and positive affirmation of the important role you play in the life of your child. The world at large may continue view children living in the autism disorder spectrum as being different and may require more time to accept them as "normal" human beings, but as far as I'm concerned, they'll always be *Uniquely Made* just as the Lord intended them to be.

Freeman L. Semons, Jr.
Milwaukee, Wisconsin 2016

"There are no ordinary people—we were created to be unique."

— Dave Branon

Uniquely Made

Chapter One

Walking a Mile in My Shoes

I am the custodial parent of three children and the caregiver of two autistic sons. Their names are Elijah and Emmanuel. Elijah is the older one of the two. My oldest and only daughter Khaila wasn't born with autism but she has proven to be special and uniquely made in her own right. I'll speak more about Khaila and the significant role she continues to play in the lives of her younger brothers later in the book.

As stated, both Elijah and Emmanuel have autism but at different sides of the spectrum. Emmanuel is the higher functioning one of the pair, mainly because his developmental and cognitive delays were detected at a much earlier age than the similar delays found in Elijah. Because of this, Emmanuel has been able to excel academically in areas where Elijah still struggles, but not to the point where it interferes with or hinders his ability to learn.

Elijah can be somewhat of an introvert at times, but regardless of that trait, he is very intelligent (especially when it comes to tinkering with computer technology), very musically inclined (he has perfect vocal pitch as well as a strong desire to create music via instruments) and possesses an ever-growing need to understand the world around him as best as his level of comprehension allows. He is currently sixteen years old (at the time I wrote this book) and stands at 6’2’’ (a gentle giant to all for lack of a better term) but his view of the world around him is currently that of a seven or eight year old. He has zero interests in the things teenagers his age are into (although he is starting to get into today’s hip hop music), but he does know how to have fun all the same. He loves to dance and move around (especially when playing any of the *Just Dance* video games on the Nintendo Wii console), loves to bowl as well as go to places like Chucky E. Cheese or Dave & Buster's, and likes to watch televisions shows like Blue's Clues, Little Einsteins, Yo Gabba Gabba, Word Girl, Daniel Tiger's Neighborhood and Dora the Explorer to name a few. Elijah can be extremely affectionate when he wants to be. He still likes to kiss me on the cheek at bedtime, gives me hugs regularly and tells me he loves me numerous times throughout any given day. When it comes to things like the simple expression of his own personal thoughts, he isn't always able to achieve it. This isn't due to a lack of effort on his part, mind you. It simply comes from a cognitive inability to formulate the right word usage to make his thoughts and/or emotional expression known to me or others at the appropriate moments.

Emmanuel is much more of an extrovert, overly active to a hyper degree and the verbally expressive one between the two boys. Emmanuel, or Manny as he is sometimes called, has the mind of a builder, the imagination of a storyteller, the soul of an explorer and the heart of a cheerful giver. As previously mentioned, Manny is doing very well in school with only minor difficulties. At age 13 (and currently in the 8th grade), he is at a 5th grade level in all academics and is especially good with math and reading. For example, you can ask him things like "What's 7 times 4?" or "What's 12 times 10?" and without any delay in thought, he'll give you the correct answer every time. I should mention that Emmanuel is very passionate about trains (i.e. Thomas the Tank Engine) and cars (Hot Wheels) and makes sure everyone he interacts with knows it as well. He likes to line his trains and cars up in a perfect formation (a very common autistic trait) and even likes to carry some of them around with him as a form of familiarity to provide him with a sense of security (especially when going to new places). Much like Elijah, Emmanuel is very computer literate, has perfect vocal pitch (he loves to sing whenever possible), likes the same Nick Jr television shows as his brother, love to engage in outdoor activities (like bike riding or roller blading) and possesses an equally ever-growing need to understand the world around him by asking numerous questions on a wide range of topics related to his overall interests and development.

Both boys have hearts of gold, possess a positive yet optimistic view on life in general and are very friendly towards everyone they meet, almost to a fault. This has much to do with the way each boy processes common human interactions as well as the world around them in terms of their individual sensory input. Elijah and Emmanuel have also displayed excellent recall abilities and can draw on past memories, places they have been to or events in perfect detail. Repetition (or the joy of it) is another common thing with each of them. Whether it's the constant rewinding of a favorite scene from one of their Nick Jr shows on the DVR or the repeating of certain words and phrases they draw comfort from, it's just a part of who they are. Neither Elijah nor Emmanuel have a sense of danger and would approach anyone (no matter who they are) to give friendly greetings or to simply ask them questions of a curious nature over anything else. Both boys are constantly being taught proper social interactions and cues (either through me, through other family members or through their respective teachers/educators) because of their tendency to invade someone's personal space and/or interrupt a conversation that may be taking place around them.

Here's a little history on how my path to fatherhood began and when signs of the boys' respective autistic conditions were first detected: I was thirty going on thirty-one when I met and married the kids' mother. Although my ex-wife had two teenage children of her own at the time of our initial meeting, it wasn't until my daughter Khaila was born in 1997 that I became a full-fledged father. Three years after Khaila's birth, Elijah was born in 2000, and three years following that, Emmanuel was born in 2003. There were no major complications with Khaila's birth and only a few with Emmanuel's birth but with Elijah's birth, there was one noteworthy complication worth mentioning. Elijah was born several weeks before his expected due date. There were no signs of any birth defects or deformities when it came to Elijah's overall wellbeing. He grew and developed as any newborn child did, but in hindsight of that unforeseen event, his earlier than expected birth would serve as a precursor of sorts for what was to come.

As children growing up in the household, I had took it upon myself to videotape my children's early childhood experiences and adventures in addition to taking as many pictures as I could for when the occasion called for it. Khaila was about ten months old when I started the family video journal. Elijah was five months when I started filming him and as far as Emmanuel was concerned, I was able to capture his live birth on video. I didn't realize the importance of keeping a family video journal of the kids at the time, but as time passed and progressed, it become something of a valuable treasure all three children, especially the boys, came to appreciate immensely as they got older. The family videos I made also allowed me and my ex-wife to see something we never thought to expect when it came to Elijah's cognitive development. You see, for all intents and purposes, Elijah was developing as a newborn child was supposed to. He learned to crawl, eat, suck his bottle, makes common baby sounds, walk and behave as an infant would, but all of that would change by the time he turned two years old.

After Elijah turned two, he became very quiet and non-verbal. Any sounds of communication he used to make prior to turning age two just stopped suddenly without any kind of warning beforehand. My ex-wife and I didn't think anything of it at first but as time went on, we would learn about it soon enough. It wasn't until Elijah started K-3 that we learned of his potential autistic condition from one of his instructors. Like many parents who have found themselves in the same predicament and confronted with such life-altering information, both my ex-wife and I were devastated by the news. We even went through a state of denial for a time, but eventually and through much soul searching, I was finally able to reach a place where I continued to love, accept and appreciate Elijah for who he was regardless of the possibility of him being autistic. He was my first born son after all and he would always hold a special place in my heart no matter what.

By the time Emmanuel turned two and started displaying similar cognitive developmental delays as Elijah had two years prior, both boys underwent an official assessment evaluation and it was determined that each of them did indeed have a form of the autism spectrum disorder. It was also around that time the boys started seeing a behavioral physiologist to help my ex-wife and I better manage their autistic conditions in addition to receiving speech therapy and other related curriculum as a part of their respective Individualized Education Programs provided by Milwaukee Public Schools.

I would like to state that I never wanted Elijah and Emmanuel to start taking or using any kind of medications like Vyvanse, Risperidone or Abilify at such young ages because of the potential health risk involved (I'll speak more about this in a moment). Over a period of seven years after the boys were diagnosed, I've had the personal privilege of communicating with parents who opted not to use any kind of medications as well as parents who made the ultimate choice to use medications as a means of helping them cope with the stresses and challenges that come with raising special needs children. My ex-wife and I fell in the latter category.

The medications Elijah and Emmanuel took worked as they were supposed to with only a few setbacks (especially when they wore off during the course of any given day). As time went on and the overwhelming demands of raising two autistic boys took a more paramount place in our daily lives, my ex-wife inability to deal with or handle our sons' autistic conditions became increasing evident in the way she chose to interact with them (especially during the final seven years of our marriage and even after divorce). I was the one expected to keep the boys under control whenever we attended family or social functions. I was also the one who would take the boys (Khaila included) everywhere I went (whether it was food shopping, down to the lakefront or partaking in other recreational events) because I wasn't ashamed to be seen in public with them. I made this choice for two very important reasons. The first was to give me a better understanding and sense of what to expect from the boys in a public setting to adapt accordingly. The second was to make their childhood remained as normal and as stable as possible.

I would like to take this time to touch on some of the potentially dangerous, destructive and harmful situations and/or behaviors I've had to face, manage, handle or deal with since becoming a single parent. I'll start with Emmanuel first.

Emmanuel has a very curious nature about everything and it has put him in harm's way more times than can be counted. Emmanuel can also be mischievous and sneaky when he wants to be, especially when it comes to taking things that don't belong to him (more on this in a moment). When he was a toddler, Emmanuel climbed up on the kitchen table and attacked an innocent apple pie by devouring it with a big, goofy smile on his face. When he was a little older, Emmanuel took it upon himself to dig as many holes as he could in the backyard (much to my irritation when it came to cutting the lawn) earning him the well deserved nickname "residential geologist".

Much of the funny, crazy things Manny did (both past and present) were innocent in nature but as he approached his pre-teen years, he started doing some strange things that put him (and us) at risk of potential life-threatening harm. One particular incident that happened two summers ago involved Emmanuel messing with one of the electrical outlets in the bedroom he shares with Elijah to the point where accidently he broke it, exposed the wires within and almost got electrocuted in the process. That same day, Emmanuel had also been messing with the stove and caused gas to fill the house. If I had not turned off the gas when I did or subsequently repaired the damaged power outlet later in the day, the house would have exploded as a result of Emmanuel's tampering. Needless to say, I had to educate Emmanuel extensively on the dangers of messing around with electrical outlets and the gas stoves (mainly by example as well as the use of some picture cues) before he finally understood it.

Because Emmanuel has the mind of a builder, he got into the very dangerous habit of playing with sharp knives, hammers and galvanized roofing nails to build things. These activities (which resulted in him cutting himself accidentally a few times too many) have been secured and brought under control for the most part but continue to remain under constant observation nevertheless for Emmanuel's safety and protection.

Emmanuel also went through a brief destructive phase where he was purposely putting holes into the basement walls for no particular reason at all. This behavior was brought to an immediate end (once I became aware of it) and I am happy to report that there haven't been any more vandalism incidents to our home on Manny's part since.

There is something else I should mention concerning Emmanuel before shifting my thoughts back on Elijah. The kids' mother made me aware of some of the incendiary remarks Emmanuel has been saying towards her whenever the kids are with her on her designated weekends. Emmanuel told her (on more than one occasion) that she isn't his mother anymore as well as some other things related to it. She informed me she was hurt by that kind of talk and wanted to know why he would say such things. I informed her Emmanuel is feeling left out and needs her to play a more active, involving role in his life outside the obligatory two to three weekends out of each month. My ex-wife has since remarried and that is something the boys continue to adjust to on a daily basis. In my continuing efforts to help Emmanuel adjust, handle and understand why his mother and I aren't together anymore, I tell him his mother will always be his mother just as I'll always be his father. In his heart, Emmanuel knows what I tell him is true but there will always be a part of him that just wants his mom and dad back together again.

When it comes to Elijah, things aren't quite as severe or extreme as they have been with Emmanuel, but he does have his moments nevertheless. Elijah has a wandering, restless spirit. He likes to wander and explore his surroundings (especially at places like Wal-Mart and Woodman's). Because Elijah isn't able to share his thoughts or make them known to all in the way that Emmanuel does, his mind can become so overloaded and cluttered by daily sensory input to the point where even his attempts at peaceful slumber is greatly affected by it (think of shaking a bottle of soda but not removing the cap to release it). As a result, Elijah has a regular habit of waking up in the middle of the night and wandering around in the house (even with the sleep medication he takes nightly). This nocturnal activity not only affects Elijah getting a decent night of sleep, it also affects my ability to achieve it as well. There have been many nights where I would get woken up by Elijah's restlessness. Some nights I'm able to get him to go back to bed with some minor redirection before going back to bed myself, some nights I can't and we both end up losing out on getting proper sleep. This is something I continue to work on with Elijah because there have been a few incidents where he has actually wandered outside the home and was seen walking around (a neighbor informed me she saw him outside in the early morning hours while on her way to work). I don't need to tell you how alarmed I was to learn that. With Elijah being a large kid standing over six feet tall, he could very easily be mistaken for a grown man by patrolling police officers or anyone else out and about during those dark predawn hours. Last thing I need is for any harm to come to Elijah due to his nocturnal wanderings. So to counteract this activity, I had to install alarms on the front and back doors for his protection just in case.

Elijah also has a somewhat insatiable appetite (which is not entirely his fault). One of the medications Elijah was prescribed early on in 2006 was Abilify. Abilify was used to help manage the irritability, aggression, mood swings, and temper tantrums that came with Elijah's autistic condition. At age seven, Elijah was a boney kid but over the course of six years, his weight, appetite and restlessness grew exponentially. This was a direct result of his Abilify usage. By the time Elijah was taken off of Abilify at age 13 and prescribed different medications to better manage his autistic condition, the damage had already been done. Let me back up a bit. In 2004, I was diagnosed with having diabetes. In 2012 (during the final months of my marriage), I made the life-changing decision to lose weight and adopt a more active, healthier lifestyle to better manage my diabetic condition for the sake of my children. In 2014, I was informed by a pediatric endocrinologist that Elijah was at risk of developing diabetes and needed to adopt a healthier lifestyle to prevent it from happening. Having autism already made Elijah's life challenging enough as is. The last thing he needed was to have diabetes thrown into the mix so I made the necessary changes towards Elijah's overall health and wellbeing right way by monitoring his daily caloric intake (the same way I do for myself) and limiting the amount of carbs he consumed on any given day. The good news here is Elijah loves to drink water (unlike Emmanuel who I will speak more about in a moment) as well as staying active (bike riding, walking, dancing) and it certainly helps. The bad news though is Elijah loves his carbs (pizza, potato chips, pasta, cake, bread, etc.) and that's where the daily challenges of keeping him healthy presented me with the most difficulty. If Elijah had an appetite like Emmanuel (a picky eater, by all accounts, who doesn't eat things like bread, cake or pizza), this would be a non issue but such is not the case. I've had to decrease the amount of snack foods I used to purchase over the past two years and replace them with healthy fruits like apples, bananas and grapes. Any snack foods I do buy have to be monitored regularly and locked up immediately because of the boys' continuous attempts to steal them while I'm sleeping, outside doing yard work or downstairs doing laundry. It's a constant battle to maintain the proper balance in the home. It really is. Some days I'm able to succeed in achieving it, some days I don't. It's all trial and error when it comes right done to it, but with each new day, I get another opportunity to get it right.

Theft and the stealing of things outside the home as well as within the home is something else each boy has had an issue with. For the longest time, any attempts I made to get Elijah and Emmanuel to understand that stealing was wrong (whether it was at Wal-Mart, at school, in my room, in Khaila's room or at someone's house) did little to halt this illicit behavior in them. It was very frustration not being able to reach them in the way I wanted to but I would soon learn of another way to diminish this behavior over time through a very simple technique. Through the advice of a psychologist Elijah was scheduled to see in the early months of 2016 (Emmanuel was also present for the session), he explained it to me like this: "Before going to a place like Wal-Mart, bring something along with you that each boy values. This could be something as simple as a toy, a stuffed animal or even a DVD. Inform each boy that if they take something that doesn't belong to them, you will keep the object they value and they won't get it back." The purpose of this technique was to get Elijah and Emmanuel to understand (on a very basis level) that stealing of any kind was wrong. Simply telling them that stealing is wrong just didn't work. I know because I have tried it many times before to no avail. With this new technique, however, all of that had changed for the better. Once the boys finally came to understand the potential risk of lose something they greatly valued by taking things that didn't belong to them, it opened the door to better communication and understanding between us.

With the nurturing and caregiving that goes along with raising Elijah and Emmanuel, there is no such thing as a dull or boring moment. It just doesn't exist in our household. They definitely keep me on my toes at all times and I sometimes have to sleep with the proverbial one eye open to ensure the quality of care they've grown accustomed to receiving (especially over the past five years) remains consistent throughout the entire process. It can be very overwhelming, highly demanding and extremely stressful to say the least but through God's grace and favor (I will speak more about this in greater detail in the appropriate chapter), I continue to receive the daily strength needed to be the parent my boys so rightly deserve.

Chapter Two

Structure, Routine & Autistic Characteristics

In the 1988 hit movie *Rain Man*, there is a very memorable scene of an autistic savant named Raymond (portrayed masterfully by actor Dustin Hoffman) adhering to a strict daily structure and routine. While traveling cross country to Los Angeles with his abrasive and selfish younger brother Charlie (Tom Cruise), Raymond informed him that it was almost time for Judge Wapner to come on. Before Charlie came to know he had an older brother or subsequently removed him from the mental institution he had lived in for much of his life, Raymond would watch People's Court every weekday at

3:30 pm without fail. When the potential of missing People's Court that day came close to becoming a reality, Raymond immediately became distressed by it and started having a meltdown. If Charlie hadn't convinced a Midwest family to let Raymond watch People's Court on their television out of the kindness of their hearts, Raymond's meltdown would've gone from bad to worst.

Structure and routine is something the average person doesn't really give much thought to when it comes to day to day living but it's something we all continue to live by whether we choose to admit it or not. We wake up. We tend to our personal hygienic needs. We eat meals and drink liquids throughout the course of the day. We attend school. We work. We interact and socialize with our peers. We shop. We pay our bills, and at the end of each day, we sleep. To a normal person, that kind of structure and routine is very commonplace when it comes to living the life we have all been given, but to a person living with autism, structure and routine takes on a whole different meaning altogether.

Elijah lives by a more stringent routine code than Emmanuel does. Here's a list of some of the things Elijah does throughout the course of any given day as it relates to his regular routine and autistic tendencies:

1. Elijah will open the window blinds in the living room, in the kitchen and in various other rooms in the house every morning to let the light in. He will do this without fail whether the sun is shining or not.
2. When Elijah is watching his favorite shows on the television or engaged in his regular fun-filled activities on the computer, on his iPad or on the Wii console, he doesn't want anyone to be around him. If someone does come into the room or invade the place in the house he occupies, he will immediately turn off the device (if it's the television or the computer) and go to a different place in the house (namely the rec room in the basement where he can access the second Wii console in solitude). If Elijah is on his iPad, he will simply take it with him to another room to achieve solitude once more. There have been many instances where Emmanuel would want to watch the same shows as his brother on the television in the living room but Elijah won't allow it. He has had minor to major meltdowns when he feels his solitude is being threatened and would call for me to tell Emmanuel to leave the room. On the flip side of all of that, there have been many instances where Elijah would play tag with either Emmanuel or Khaila (whenever she's home from college) whenever he is in a more sociable, jovial and interactive mood.

3. At times when we would go out somewhere, like Wal-Mart, Woodman's or even at their school, Elijah will always walk ahead of me and Emmanuel rather than walk side by side with us. This kind of standoffish activity isn't just restricted to walking. Because I currently work as a school bus driver (mainly because of the flexibility of schedule it gives me) and my second route is the boys school, they are able to ride with me to and from their school. Elijah would sit as far away from Emmanuel while on the bus and has made it a habit to move to different seats several times several times until he feels comfortable. He is also known for making unexpected loud sounds and phrases and even raises an open hand to one side of his face while sporting a happy yet goofy facial expression. I've come to view this as Elijah's way of thinking out loud due to some of the things he would say in those moments. Most of it comes from the television shows he likes to watch while the other things he would say comes from him imitating something he may have heard or saw throughout the course of the day.
4. Elijah has a habit of repeating things to get my attention. It doesn't matter if we're at home, on the school bus or in the car. Here's a quick example: If I tell Elijah we have to go to the store after I get off work, he would come back later saying "Go to the store, Dad" several

times before I'm able to get him to understand that we'll be going to the store just like I told him the first time.

5. Elijah likes to ramble on about things familiar to him as a means of comfort. This activity usually happens when he is upset, nervous, scared or agitated about something.
6. Elijah will remind me when to give him and Emmanuel their pm medications at 7 o'clock without fail. He doesn't need to look at a clock while doing this; he always goes by his internal clock. While on the subject of time, Elijah has no real concept of what daylight savings time is (or Manny for that matter) and during the six months of the year it's in effect, he would remind me about their pm medications an hour earlier than the usual time until his internal clock has adjusted accordingly.

Emmanuel's daily activities fall more in line with typical routines he has developed over a long period of time. Here's a short list of his usual routines and autistic tendencies worth mentioning:

1. Emmanuel has made it a routine to eat each portion of a meal separately as opposed to eating everything together. For example, if Manny is eating pancakes and bacon, he will eat the pancakes first (with lots of syrup, of course) before eating the bacon. With Emmanuel especially, his food consumption is based on the texture of the food itself, which is

a fairly common trait associated with someone who has autism. This is also why Emmanuel is such a picky eater. If a particular food item doesn't have the right look or texture to it, Emmanuel won't eat it. In order to get him to try different foods at the appropriate meal times, I would have to introduce them to him gradually over time until he became more accustomed to eating them. At one point, Manny would only eat certain things, particularly when it came to things like Reese's Peanut Butter cereal, Banquet Salisbury Steak meals and Chef Boyardee's spaghetti rings with meatballs cup meals. As of today, Emmanuel's overall food consumption has greatly improved. Once I became aware of how significant food texture plays into the things he would or would not eat, it made it easier for Emmanuel to try out different foods without resistance.

2. Emmanuel has made it a habit to think out loud in the same manner that Elijah does but unlike his older brother, Emmanuel is more articulate (and at times unfiltered) with his thoughts and his words. He also likes to laugh out loud at something he found extremely funny or amusing. If it's a scene from one of the Nick Jr shows or a Nickelodeon DVD for example, Emmanuel will replay it over and over again, laughing and giggling while doing so. Emmanuel has also been known to ramble or

mumble his thoughts in a low vocal tone. He usually does this when he doesn't get his way.

3. Emmanuel likes to ask numerous questions throughout any given day. The answers the questions he likes to ask the most are already known to him but he continues to ask them any way.
4. During the warm months of the year, Emmanuel likes to spend much of it outside (like clockwork) whenever possible to roller blade, ride bike or just play with his toys. This is something I've come to expected out of him and I continue to do what I must to stay in shape so that I can keep up with him.

Here's a list of other common autistic characteristics exhibited by both Elijah and Emmanuel throughout the course of their continuing development:

1. Have a good memory

2. Learns very well through picture cues (as stated in the previous chapter)

3. Very accepting of others

4. Have lots of energy (Emmanuel especially)

5. Do not always making eye contact with their peers

6. Plays with their toys differently than other kids

7. Giggles or smiles a lot (as previously mentioned)

8. Prefer to be alone (more common with Elijah than Emmanuel)

9. Do not like loud noises (very common with both boys)

10. Will sometimes play with others as well as play in solitude

11. Performs best when following an established schedule

12. Knows lots of quotes (saying) from favorite TV shows and movies

During the time I served in the Marine Corps, I came to learn the importance of establishing the proper structured schedule as an effective means of time management to ensure the right balance is always maintained throughout the course of any given day. Here's a detailed list of the structured schedule I currently have in place as it relates to the boys' overall care and hygienic needs:

Brush Teeth (Oral Hygiene)	Done daily
Getting Dressed	Done daily
Wash ups	2 to 3 times per week
Showers	3 to 4 times per week
Hot Breakfast	3 to 4 times per week

Cold Breakfast	2 to 3 times per week
Lunch (At Home or at School)	Done daily
Afternoon Snack	Done daily
Dinner	Done daily
Boys Haircuts	2 to 3 times per month
Cutting the Boys' Fingernails & Toe Nails	2 to 3 times per month
Medical Physicals	Once a year
Dental Appointments	Twice a year
Psychiatric Appointments	Every 3 to 4 months
Endocrinologist Appointments (Elijah)	Twice a year
Hygiene Inspections	Done daily
Eye Appointments	Once a year
Medications	Received & taken daily

When it come to things like teeth brushing, getting dressed, taking showers, washing ups and wiping after using the bathroom, both Elijah and Emmanuel had to be taught very extensive on how to properly perform each task required of them over a long period of time. Hygiene picture cues found online throughout the years have been a great help in this area and has made it much easier for both boys to understand how to perform these tasks on their own with minimum supervision involved. There are still times though when I have to step in to supervise to make sure they're doing their daily task correctly and it's something I continue to address/monitor as each situation arises.

Probably the biggest and most life-altering change Elijah and Emmanuel have had to face during the course of their respective young lives thus far came to them in the form of divorce. My seventeen year marriage ended in the worst way imaginable, but through God's abiding love, grace and favor, I've been able to rise above the heart shattering experience to heal, move on and continue being the parent my children need me to be. Khaila did have some issues early on in the divorce process that needed to be addressed right away, but since then, she too has overcome the emotional experience through much counseling, prayer and support. The boys, on the hand, didn't adjust or come to accept to the new status quo as well as their sister had been able to and it had much to do with their respective autistic conditions over anything else.

For Elijah, the divorce process as a whole was harder for him to deal with than it was for Emmanuel. He wasn't able to share his thoughts or feelings about it but he found another way to make the internal pain he was experiencing known to me nevertheless. During the first six to seven months, Elijah went through bouts of crying at home as well as at school. The times he would cry at home usually happened before bedtime or during the middle of the night after he had been sleeping for a few hours. In those moments, I would comfort him in the best ways possible by giving him a hug, wiping away his tears and telling him everything is going to be alright. Whenever I would ask him “what’s wrong?” all he could tell me was “I’m sad”. As mentioned, Elijah would experience emotional outburst while in school as well. His teachers (at the time) brought it to my attention during a parent/teacher’s conference and asked if there had been any significant changes taking place in the home that would cause Elijah to have tearful outburst like that out of the blue. When I informed them of the divorce, Elijah’s teachers immediately understood the situation and continued to offer him words of comfort and support whenever those moments would occur. With regards to Emmanuel, I touched on some of the ways the divorce affected him in the previous chapter and would like to expand on it at this time.

When I was a child, I watched my own parents go through a painful divorce. I was ten going on eleven and I can still remember how the whole experience made me feel inside. Feelings of sadness, loss, anxiety and fear were chief among the range of emotions I experienced at the time and it was something I had to go through on my own. My mother, God rest her soul, did her best to help me and my siblings cope with her divorce from my father but ongoing parental responsibilities coupled with some life-threatening medical conditions (two brain tumors that ultimately lead to partial paralysis after removal) had often interfered with that process. My mother never allowed those obstacles to stop her from being the parent we needed her to be during those turbulence times and I have come to greatly benefit from her parental examples of selflessness, dedication, commitment and sacrifice since becoming a single parent.

Khaila's continued presence in the household has been a blessing and has made the transition from a two parent home to a single parent home much easier for the boys to handle and process. She could have very well gone to live with her mother during the separation process but I am glad she made the decision to stay. She knows her brothers almost as well as I do and it continues to shine through in the way she interacts with them. As far as Elijah and Emmanuel are concerned, Khaila is their loving sister (although Manny thinks she is a bully lol), a motherly figure to them in so many ways and the one sibling who continues to accept them just as they are.

Another aspect of divorce is co-parenting and the establishing of a balanced schedule that works towards maintaining a good stable foundation for every child involved.

Here are the numbers for the co-parenting schedule as it presently stands:

Time Spent with Dad	Time Spent with Mom
313 days out of the year	52 days out of the year (Designated Weekends)

I decided to reveal these numbers to further illustrate the great imbalance that currently exist when it comes to the time the boys spend with me throughout the year and the time they would spend with their mother.

For the first two years after the marriage end in 2012, the time Elijah and Emmanuel would spend with their mother was much less than the 52 days shown above. Some improvement has been made in this area over the last three years but not by much and it only adds to the fact of how Elijah and Emmanuel—in their own unique ways, have felt completely left out of their mother's new life. Now, to my ex-wife's credit, she does spend time with the boys on their respective birthdays as well as Thanksgiving, Christmas and other family gatherings, which is always important, but nothing more outside of that.

In accordance to the divorce decree, the kids' mother is also required to take the boys two evenings out of the weeks she doesn't have them for the weekend. This still hasn't happened as of yet and at this juncture, I seriously doubt it will ever happen, largely due in part to consistent non involvement into the daily affairs of our sons. When it comes to co-parenting after divorce, each parent has a duty and a responsibility to spend an equal amount of quality time with their children to ensure that their emotional needs, wants and concerns remain paramount throughout the entire co-parenting experience. To do anything less than that would cause the children involved to feel like they don't matter much in the eyes of the absent parent who chooses not to be there during those crucial moments of childhood development and has the potential of causing irreparable psychological damage over time.

Schedule imbalances like this, especially when it comes to the co-parenting of special needs children, isn't uncommon in today's society. It's something that happens more times than naught (usually at the custodial parent's expense) and has become increasing more common with each passing year with no signs of slowing down. At one point, it was the father who often left or abandoned their kids (special needs or otherwise) to seek new life beyond the boundaries of a martial or romantic relationship, but not so anymore. Mothers of special needs children are now the ones doing it at such an alarming degree that it overshadows any father who still chooses to leave the bulk of the parental care in the hands of the other parent. In most of these instances, the parents who are left to raise their special needs child (or children) alone aren't given much choice or say so in the matter. I know I wasn't given one, but in light of that, it has never given me any cause or reason to regret the important role I continue to have in the lives of my children and it never will.

Adaptation and change are two things that don't come easy to children living with autism. Both Elijah and Emmanuel tend to stick to familiar things that continue to bring them comfort, refuge, peacefulness and happiness as opposed to venturing into unfamiliar territory. Elijah still likes to play with preschool toys and video games and still likes to watches preschool television programs because of his familiarity of such things. At the time Elijah originally engaged in those activities from age two to six, there were two parents in the home in addition to his older siblings as well. Life for Elijah was less complicated, much simpler and not marred with the many household changes that have occurred over the last twelve years. I've come to view this as Elijah's way of holding on to the treasured memories of the past without losing sight of what they mean to him and how they continue to define him as a person. For Emmanuel, sticking to the things that are familiar to him has made it somewhat difficult for him to connect with children in his age group on a social level. Because Emmanuel still likes to talk about Thomas the Tank Engine and discuss his favorite Nick Jr or Disney Jr television shows, he would often get confusing looks from any teenager he tries speak to about them. More often than naught, Emmanuel finds it easier to have conversations with kids much younger than him, but even in that regard, some of the younger kids don't always feel inclined to talk to him about such things because they will always view him as a "big kid".

The unique space that Elijah and Emmanuel occupy is a place most kids in their respective age groups know nothing about. Elijah and Emmanuel may be teenagers in age but they are not bound by it. Their individual views of the world around them have allowed them to embrace and hold on to the innocent things most people living outside of the autism disorder spectrum tend to let go of as they grow older. There is a genuine purity of heart, mind and soul residing within Elijah and Emmanuel that simply doesn't exist in kids who are considered to be normal. Those words (from the previous sentence) have been said to me on more than one occasion by their Special Ed educators (both past and current) as well as from the people who have had the fortune of interacting with them. Raising normal teenagers can be challenging in ways that are both common and familiar, but with Elijah and Emmanuel, the word challenge is just another word for exploration, and where we go from here will always be determined by their willingness to stay true to who God created them to be.

Chapter Three

Sensory Input, Overloads & Perceptions

Imagine, for a moment, that all of your senses have been cranked up way beyond the normal acceptable levels you've grown accustomed to and you were still expected to behave as you always have in the midst of it. How do you think it would affect your interaction with the world around you? How would you cope with being able to see, hear, touch, taste or even smell things far beyond the capacity of the average person? Would you be able to handle it without difficulty or would the sheer thought of having amplify senses overwhelm you to the point of madness? To a person living with autism, having acute, sensitive or even heighten senses of sight, smell, touch, taste and hearing is something that just comes with the experience. I have noticed keen senses activity in both Elijah and Emmanuel over the years. For Emmanuel, this activity has been very evident with his hearing, his sense of touch and his sense of taste. For Elijah, this activity has become exceedingly obvious in all of his five senses at one point or another.

In the previous chapter, I touched on how texture has much to do with the way Emmanuel picks and choose the things he likes to eat. Texture (or rather tactile contact) as a whole doesn't stop there with him. Everything from the clothes he wears right down to his socks and the shoes on his feet have to have the right feel to them. If they don't have the right feel about them, it would cause Emmanuel to experience serious discomfort to the point where he would take off his shirt or socks no matter where he may be to achieve the desired level of comfort once more. Emmanuel has been known to get hot very easily and it continues to play a factor into his decision making as well. In terms of Emmanuel's hearing, it is very acute. I can remember one morning when he was complaining about a bird outside the window singing too loud. I could hear the same bird singing but the bird in question was almost three to four houses away from us. Emmanuel does own a pair of noise reduction headphones that has helps to cancel out any extraneous sounds threatening to cause him any immediate discomfort while allowing him to better focus on the things he really wants to hear.

With Elijah, his hearing is just as acute as Emmanuel but he is able to filter out loud sounds without the use of noise reduction headphones. Elijah's sense of taste is particularly strong. When it comes to eating, it is almost a euphoric experience him in many ways (especially when eating his favorite foods) and he has been known to hum during intake consumption. Elijah is able to smell things better than others and will let you if he smells something that doesn't agree with him. Elijah doesn't like to be touched sometimes and will put as much space as he deems necessary to avoid being bumped into or in close contact with his peers. If he feels his personal space is being compromised, Elijah immediately becomes defensive, agitated or even distressed as a result of it. Elijah's eyesight remains exceptionally good (even with having to wear glasses) and he continues to benefit from it. Both boys have to wear glasses but Elijah didn't have to start wearing them until 2016. Elijah can still see things at a great distance. For example, whenever I take the boys to familiar places (like the Goodwill, Chucky E. Cheese or Stonefire Pizza Co.), Elijah automatically knows where we are going by seeing familiar landmarks in the distance during the trip. There is a good reason why Elijah (and Emmanuel as well) are able to do this and I'll take this time to explain.

Each day Elijah and Emmanuel wake up and go about their usual business throughout the course of a typical day, their individual brains are constantly recording, processing and storing all sensory input data that comes to them by way of their five senses. If Elijah and Emmanuel receive a steady amount of sensory input, they're able to function just fine in the world around them but if they receive too much sensory input due to an increase of sounds, sights or activities, it can cause a disruption in their daily functioning that could potentially lead to a sensory input overload. People considered normal are able to adjust, filter, adapt or avoid any sensory input that threatens to overload their senses without much fanfare but those same common instincts don't always come so easy to a person living in the autism disorder spectrum.

The sensory input process Elijah and Emmanuel undergo throughout the day can easily be divided into three categories: *minimum, medium and maximum.*

Here's a layout of how the three sensory input categories work and play into one another:

Minimum Sensory Input
Happens in places of great familiarity
i.e. Home (where major changes are minimal at best)

Medium Sensory Input
Happens in places of continuous familiarity
i.e. School (where changes are fairly moderate)

Maximum Sensory Input
Happens in places of great unfamiliarity
i.e. Public Places (where major changes are commonplace)

Home will always be the one place where daily sensory input for Elijah and Emmanuel remains nominal, steady and well maintained. The house in which we live is the only home the boys know since birth and the one place they are able to draw immediate refuge from no matter the many changes life brings to them. That statement isn't meant to imply that Elijah and Emmanuel are immune from experiencing medium or maximum sensory input episodes while at home. There have been many instances where each boy has experienced sensory overloads that have lead to bouts of agitation, restlessness and distress but the sources of those sensory overloads are easily identified and resolved as quickly as they occur. The sensory input episodes that happen in public place, and even at school, often take more time and effort to resolve.

I can recall a few times where each boy has received way too much sensory input information. Places like Six Flags Great America or special events like the Tripoli Shrine Circus, seasonal church carnivals and 4th of July fireworks celebrations can prove to be extremely demanding on their acute senses. It's something that I have to continue to be very mindful of whenever I take the boys to places or events they had never been to or experienced before.

While it's in thought, I do need to mention that Elijah and Emmanuel continue to show great improvement in the way they manage their sensory perceptions as they grow older. Yes, there still are some challenges to be sure, but knowing each of my sons as well as I do has afforded me the confidence and the opportunity to help navigate them through these overload sensory difficulties better than someone completely unfamiliar with their respective autistic tendencies.

Another area of sensory perception that often gets overlooked when it comes to children living and growing up in the autism disorder spectrum is puberty. Just as cognitive and developmental delays come with the affects of autism, puberty development can face the same delays. Puberty for Elijah didn't start until he was fourteen going on fifteen. For Emmanuel, he was thirteen going on fourteen. When Elijah puberty stages didn't start (as is common for with a child becoming a teenager), I became concerned. There was a point when I even thought Elijah had Prader-Willi syndrome. For anyone unfamiliar, Prader-Willi syndrome a rare disorder present at birth that results in a number of physical, mental and behavioral problems with children diagnosed with it. Five notable takeaways from the syndrome are *delayed intellectual development, hyperphagia, excessive weight gain, sleep disorders and delayed puberty.*

Luckily, Elijah's doctor was quick to dismiss the notion of him suffering from the syndrome effects after the proper blood work and examinations were done. Once Elijah did begin to grow in height as normal (autistic developmental delays notwithstanding) in addition to signs of hair growth on his face, under his arms, in his pubic area and a deepening of his voice, any causes for concern about the Prader-Willi syndrome effects on him no longer carried any tangible merit.

Emmanuel's puberty development, once it started, happened and progressed as it was meant to occur. Like Elijah, Emmanuel is continuing to grow tall as his puberty development continues and is expected to stand over six feet once his growing spurt progression reaches its natural conclusion. Both boys have gone through a period of trying to better understand all of the changes and sensations that come with being a teenager. I have received picture cues from the boys' teachers on the subject of puberty and it has helped in giving each boy greater grasp of what they're going through. Both boys became very much aware of the inherent differences between a boy and a girl as the stages of puberty became more evident and it has placed each of them in some rather peculiar yet interesting situations at home as well as at school.

There were a few brief isolated moments when Elijah started filming his genitals with his iPad in the bathroom and down in the basement rec area. Of course this activity was put to an end once I found out about it, but if I had to make an educated guess as to why he started doing it, curiosity over the interior and exterior changes happening to him as a result of puberty would probably be at the root of it. As for Emmanuel, he was found in the boys' restroom at school by one of his teachers touching (examining his genitals) because it had grown longer (and larger) than he had been accustomed to from years gone by. There was an isolated incident where Elijah touched the breast of a substitute teacher out of curiosity at his former school but the matter was immediately addressed and corrected to prevent it from happening again.

One of the biggest misconceptions when it comes to individuals living with autism is that they don't feel things like people considered normal or experience sensations and/or emotions the way others do. Autistic individuals are very much capable of expressing themselves and completely in tune to other people's emotions at all times, even when those expressions (when expressed) aren't always clear to them or to their peers when it comes down to the actual execution. Because of the acute sensitive of their sensory perceptions, people living in the autism disorder spectrum probably experience things to such a greater degree that they don't always know how to make sense of it all. It is for these reasons a greater level of patience, acceptance and thoughtfulness must be given (granted) in order for them to gain a better comprehension process all of the sensory changes, both internal and external, taking place around them. This is something that doesn't come easy nor is it meant to. I know when it comes to Elijah and Emmanuel; it's all about trial and error. I don't always get it right and it can be very frustrating at times when I'm unable to help them understand how to handle such things, but in those precious moments I do get it right, it makes all the effort put forth in helping them comprehend something they didn't know beforehand worthwhile in the long run.

Chapter Four

The Importance of Having a Good Support Group

I wish I could tell you that being the single parent of two special needs teens has been easy and challenge free, but I can't. I really wish I could tell you that I never considered taking my own life to put an ease to the incessant parental challenges and struggles I face daily, but I can't. What I can tell you though is throughout every challenge, trial, struggle, opposition and obstacle I have encountered or faced since becoming a single parent, God was right there with me every step of the way, fighting the battles threatening to pull me down and setting a clear path to tread upon no matter the time, day or season.

My cousin Regina recently told me that I don't know how to quit or give up and that certainly appears to be the case. My sisters Donna, Karen, Crystal and Mary in addition to many others like them have made it a point to tell me just how strong, blessed and highly favored I truly am in the eyes of the Lord.

Over the course of the past several years, I have learned some pretty hard lessons in terms of faith, family and friendships. I have come to learn who my true friends are in the midst of constant adversity and struggle and who was never a true friend to me at all. The same thing can be said about family, or rather former in-laws who once welcomed me into the fold with open arms. Divorce has a way of changing the way people choose to interact with you going forward and not always for the better. Without much warning beforehand, things like abandonment, being unfairly misjudged or forgotten altogether had suddenly become the new norm in the wake of it all and it has made for many solitary periods without the benefit of having a solid support system in place to provide much needed comfort and encouragement. The only positive take away I was able to draw from the entire experience is how it has opened the door to new and better relationships with people unbound by having to pick or choose a side to stand on.

In terms of faith, my personal relationship with God through His son Christ Jesus has become much stronger the more I seek and abide in Him. Now granted, I didn't always walk with Christ as I knew I should, especially during those dark moments when the way got especially rough and very difficult to tread. I'm also willing to admit that my thoughts and my faith in myself haven't always been on par with my best interests when God's favor was clearly upon me, but through it all, the unwavering belief I continue to have in the Lord has remained consistent in strength nevertheless. The last five years have really allowed me to see how much God has been working in my life. Not just in recent years, mind you, but throughout the entire course of my life thus far. Everything I've experienced, endured and learned along the way was meant to mold me into the person I've become today.

Another place where God has blessed me the most has to do with surrounding me with people who truly care about the well being of me and my children. These wonderful individuals, ranging from immediate family members to close friends have allowed me to vent my frustrations when needed, given me the necessary support, inspiration and encouragement to persevere, and continue to check up on me and the boys on a regular basis to make ensure all is well.

Because of everything I have gone through, I've reached a point in my life where I don't even deal with or associate with people who are so opinionated in their lack of understanding and judgment of what I seek achieve as caregiver for my boys that it skews their outlook of my overall efforts. It's so counterproductive on so many levels and it has absolutely no place or tolerance in my life. I tend to focus on the things that are important or matter the most (especially now that I'm in my fifties) because I simply do not have time to focus on things that hold no significant at all. In the previous chapter, I touched on the sensory overloads Elijah and Emmanuel have experienced from time to time. I, too, have learned that I'm prone to having mental overload episodes myself bordering on anxiety or panic attacks but not in the same capacity as my sons. Please allow me to explain this further in the next paragraph.

The caregiver role of raising special needs children alone (as you have come to discover from your reading of previous chapters) can be a very extensive and time-consuming experience. So much so that the parent (or person) doing the bulk of the caregiving can often times face severe negligence when it comes to making time for themselves, getting away to recharge or simply engaging in productive activities they enjoy doing the most. I don't always have the luxury of being able to get away from it all whenever I want to or putting my personal needs and wants above those of my children. As a result of the constant care I provide for Elijah and Emmanuel, I often times get overwhelmed more times than can be counted and have had to literally disconnect myself from all social interaction as a means of regaining some semblance of balance, clarity and harmony to continue being the steady rock of support my children count on in me at all times. It's not always an easy thing to do or achieve, especially when it comes to stay on top of everything from household management to caregiving tasks and everything in-between that has to be maintained daily. People who really don't know me all too well (and even some of the people who do) have had the audacity of criticizing me (without rightful justification, mind you) for seemingly making it all about me during highly stressful instances when I can assure you anything said or expressed on the subject couldn't be further from the truth. I have also accused me of being anti-social over the course of the past several years when I retreat into myself as opposed to reaching out to people to talk out the many stressful situations I regularly endure or go through. That, too, isn't something that always came easy as I would like because some people (quite frankly) just aren't capable of being consoling, understanding, patient, compassionate or even empathic when it really counts.

There was a period from early 2013 to mid 2015 when I made honest efforts to reach out and share my thoughts and/or feelings of frustration, doubt and isolation with anyone willing to listen but not anymore. Doing that only caused more harm than good and resulted in making me feel far worse than better about my situation. So, in an effort to prevent such counterproductive support situations like that from ever happening again, I've had to learn how to be more careful, discerning and selective when it came to building the proper support group.

My support group isn't just restricted or limited to immediate family and good friends. I have received a good level of support, inspiration and encouragement from the boys' special education teachers—both past and current—in addition to the weekly spiritual teachings I receive from the church I attend as well as a steady influx of useful resources from a collective of various special needs counselors employed through Milwaukee County and Wisconsin Promise respectively. My personal doctor has been helpful in ensuring I stay in the best health possible through regular visits made every 3 months.

I would also like to make mention of a behavioral counselor I once saw for a period of four months back in 2013 because I continue to benefit from the counsel received to this day. Here is one of the main things the behavioral counselor shared with me: He said "the best way to gauge if your life is improving in the direction you wish for it to go is to see where you are today as opposed to where you were a year ago. If you feel you are in a better place than you were a year ago mentally and emotionally, then you have made significant progress in both areas. However, if you feel you are in a worst place than you were a year ago, then there is still much progress that needs to be made."

So far, I continue to be moving in the right direction on a mental and emotional level. Sure, I still experience days where I have flashback, bad dreams or see reminders of those dark days much like a former combat soldier going through a posttraumatic stress disorder episode, but my recovery over such distressing moments has greatly improved to the point where it doesn't hinder me the way it once did. I will probably never forget or fully recover from everything that happened to get me to the place I am today. That's just the way it goes. The good news in all of it is I've become much wiser, and yes even stronger in terms of perseverance and a renewed sense of self worth, as a result.

Not too long ago, the bishop at the church I attend taught about the 3 "C"s of a father and the importance of the role as it relates to family. The 3 "C"s are "cut", "correct" and "command". Here's how it all plays out: A father cuts out the things (and/or influences) that often times threatens to interfere with the positive direction he wishes for his children to go. A father is well known for correcting his children in the appropriate moments when a wrong choice or decision has been made. I know this one very well from experiences with my own father and how it's helped shaped me into the father I am today. Lastly and even more important, a father issues commands intended to mold and shape his children for their continuous development. The 3 "C"s aren't just restricted to fathers. Mothers are also capable of performing the same functions and often do, especially when placed in positions of acting as both mother and father, but when it comes down to the role of being a father, the 3 “C”s is just a natural part of who he is in the eyes of the Lord.

Before concluding this chapter, I would be remiss if I didn’t mention the important supportive role my children have played throughout this entire single parent process. My children have kept me centered, focused and grounded on the things that matter most. Sunshine or rain, joy or pain, harmony or tribulation, my children have been there for me in ways that continue to surprise me daily as they continue to display extraordinary levels of selflessness, generosity, compassion and unconditional love far surpassing anything I’ve encountered prior to becoming a single parent. Every time I think I know everything each of them is capable of, they turn around and surprise me once more by showing me just how uniquely made they truly are. Jesus may be the source of my strength in all things (as it will always remain) but it is the absolute love I hold in my heart for my children that continue to give it the everlasting meaning and purpose it deserves.

Chapter Five

Seeing the World from Their Point of View

In April of 2016, the boys and I had been given the special privilege of attending the 27th Annual Autism Society of Wisconsin Conference. The three day event was held at the *Kalahari Resorts & Waterparks* in Wisconsin Dells from April 7th to April 9th and featured special guest speakers, a talent show, numerous exhibits, and a host of workshops geared toward raising better comprehension (awareness) of the autism condition.

Wisconsin Promise was the organization that sponsored the event for us. It was definitely time well spent for all of us. The entire experience really broadened my scope of the autism disorder spectrum as a whole and allowed me to start viewing the world the way Elijah and Emmanuel do.

The people who attended the conference ranged from Special Ed educators, behavioral therapists, and childcare providers to parents, caregivers and individuals living with autism. The conference itself provided us with a variety of strategies, tools, and resources to better aid, care and advocate for those affected by autism. So much so that many of the things I was able to learn from the numerous workshops I attended is still something being put into effectual practice to this day. One of the workshops that stood out the most and had more to do with special needs parenting overall was entitled *"Sensory Overloads vs. Behavioral Tantrums: Understanding the Difference and How to Respond"*.

The outlined objectives of the workshop designed to give all participants the necessary tools to identify signs of a sensory overload in addition to understanding differences between behavioral tantrums and said sensory overloads. During the hour or so the workshop was in session, we were presented with a full outline of the developmental stages of behavior children experience and the complete sensory system. We were also made aware of when sensory processing goes wrong (from the perspective of a special needs child to the experience every parent or caregiver encounters during the lifelong process) and that was where the information being offered to the packed room of participants benefited me the most.

When the sensory process goes wrong for a special needs child, observable responses and/or behaviors like hyper vigilance (overly guarded), aggression, fear and resistance become more evident during daily interactions. These responses and behaviors can come about as a result of being in a new environment, being separated from a familiar loved one, being exposed to new transitions or being introduced to new activities. When the sensory process goes wrong for the parent or caregiver, the parental experiences can range from difficulty reading emotional cues and hyper vigilance (over-protectiveness) to feelings of burnout, anxiety and stress from the ever-present care giving demands. Where behaviors and sensory input collide for both child and parent comes from the perception that the world is unsafe and this often opens the door to things like fear, stress and aggression. To combat those types of situations, there were a number of sensory and emotional strategies the workshop presenters touched on.

Here's the break down what they shared with us in two separate groups:

Sensory strategies involve a reduction or change in environment in an attempt to help alleviate pressure and regain a sense of calm or stability.

Emotional strategies involve recognizing the signs of fear, anxiety and aggression whenever they arise while working toward a practical resolution that benefits both child and parent.

When enacting these strategies, collaborative problem solving should always at the forefront of each step taken when it comes to prevention, processing and repair. There is much experimentation and implication that goes along with the use of these strategies, but it's all worth it for every child involved in the process. These strategies, as we were all told, are meant to work towards establishing the proper parameters over a long period of time and require a great level of patience, understanding and commitment to ensure they remain in place. The end result in all of this, of course, will eventually allow for better parent/child relations in the end and greatly reduce the amount of sensory overloads and behavioral tantrums that may occur down the road.

As I write this paragraph, a year has passed since attending the conference. Much has changed in that time. I've been able to take full advantage of the many programs I learned about from the conference, like local child care agencies for special need individuals and respite care centers, to improve our quality of living. Elijah and Emmanuel now attend a new school—Milwaukee School of Languages, where they are able to continue excelling in all area of academics. Communication has never really been an issue for Emmanuel, but this is the one area where Elijah has shown great improvement. Even though he still has yet to hold and maintain productive conversations with his peers, Elijah has found new ways to make his thoughts and expressions known to me. Whereas once he used to say "I hurt" or "I'm sad" when something was bothering him, Elijah is now able to elaborate more specifically on where and why something is hurting and why he's feeling sad. This kind of progression has filled me with an incredible sense of hope the more I continue bear witness to the significant advancement being made by each of my sons. As they continue to mature and grow, Elijah and Emmanuel have demonstrated their uncanny ability to overcome any obstacles threatening to stand in the directions they wish to go or come up against the simple goals they hope to achieve in life. I can't even begin to tell you how proud all of this makes me. My sons continue to show me that nothing is impossible through the power of belief and I will always view the level of perseverance that exists within each of them as a good thing.

Recently I had a conversation with Emmanuel about death. There is a video on YouTube he's been fixated on for some time now called "Dumb Way to Die". In the video, there is a host of charming but dumb colorful cartoon beans facing their untimely demise at the hands of the viewership in silly, humorous and stupid ways. The video even comes with a catchy theme song that Emmanuel likes to sing every chance he gets. Regular viewing of the video is what prompted Emmanuel to ask the question "Am I going to die?" My response to his innocent inquiry was "Yes." Emmanuel pressed by asking "Why?" I replied back by saying "Everyone who is born dies at some point. It's just a part of living." Emmanuel, appearing slightly downhearted, paused for a brief moment to give my response some thought. Once he had finished considering my response, Emmanuel's face immediately lit up like a well-lit Christmas tree. He soon responded cheerfully after that to say, "I'm going to ask God to let me stay alive forever."

That kind of optimistic thinking is something I've come to expect from both Emmanuel and Elijah. Anyone who has done their fair share of living knows firsthand how cruel, unfair and unforgiving the world can be. Not everyone you interact with is going to treat you with compassion or be there for you in times of need. Life can be hard sometimes. There is no doubt about it, but in the midst of hardship lies opportunity to embrace all of the positive things that continue to give life its promise and purpose. Promise and purpose is how Elijah and Emmanuel continue to view the world around them. From the conversations I've had with both boys on the subject over the years, their collective outlook on the surface can be plainly described as warm, friendly, welcoming and inviting, but it goes even deeper than that. No matter how Elijah and Emmanuel are perceived or treated by their peers, they continue to view everyone as a friend, accept them for who they are without question and always see the best in all who cross their respective paths.

I wish that everyone could see the world the way that Elijah and Emmanuel do. I really do, because if they could bring themselves, just for a moment, to envision a bright, beautiful, and colorful place where everyone is free to be whomever they choose to be and true acceptance lights up the new day like sunshine then they, regardless of creed or color, would come to discover how we are all uniquely made.

Afterword

To date, there are no known cures for autism. Although much medical research and scientific studies that have been done in pursuit of finding a cure for the disorder over the last 74 years, nothing conclusive has presented itself as of yet. There is no way of knowing if a child has autism while still in the womb or after birth, but there are a number of ways development delays can be detected, identified and diagnosed from as early as 18 months up to age 3. When it comes to the potentiality of a child being diagnosed with autism, any concerned parent should always remain proactive in every area of their child's development and take the proper early intervention steps to ensure a better outcome of the child's condition.

There have been many documented causes for autism since the term was used as an official diagnosis for 11 children studied in 1943, but from then and even up until now, nothing decisive has been found or discovered in any of studies that were conducted. Not meaning to start any conspiracy theories here but if it were up to me to take an educated guess on the probable causes for autism, the main culprits I would identify right off the bat to make my case would be our food and water supply. Not everybody receive vaccinations or has faulty genes as many scientists have made claim to through their research, but everyone does have to eat and drink as a means of survival. There have been many significant global changes over the past one hundred years in the way our food is currently being processed for consumption and our water is purified for drinking. With that being the case, there are still so many areas in the United States where families are exposed to high concentrations of lead in their tap water in addition to the many harmful (toxic) chemicals we, as a population, continue to consume in the processed foods we prepare and eat daily.

I guess when it come down to it, there really isn't a clear, concise way of knowing if any of the things I mentioned are the real causes for autism or any other related disorder like Asperger and Attention Deficit Hyperactivity Disorder (ADHD). There just isn't, at least not at the present time, but I do feel and continue to believe that it's definitely something worth further medical study by the scientific community for the sake of our children.

Family Photo Gallery

The following is collections of family photos taken from 2000 to 2017

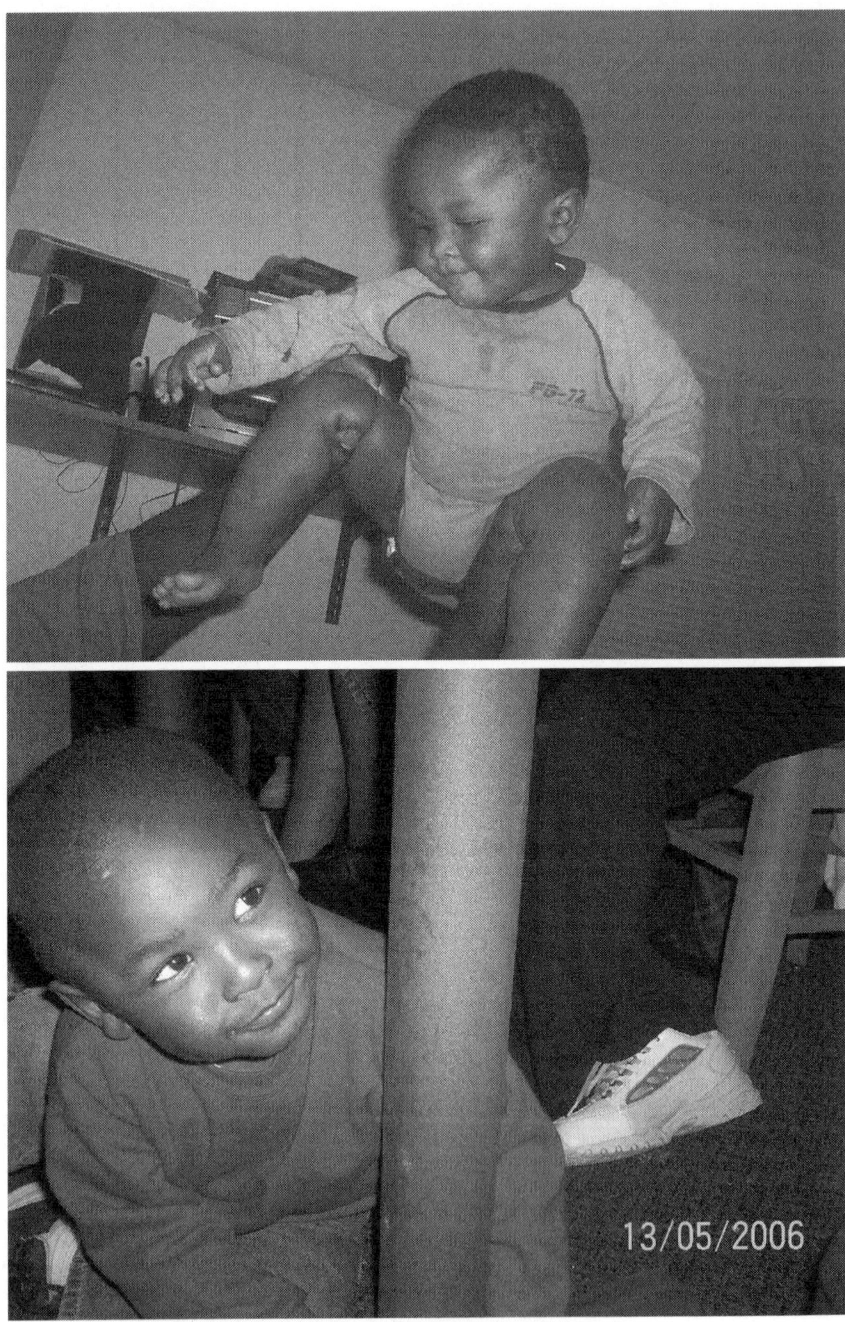
13/05/2006

Exchange
No Exchange
Propane Center

BASEBALL
LEGEND

NEESKAY

VISUAL

ELEVATOR
DASANI

17/07/2006

HELIUM
TRAMPOLINE PARK
HELP WANTED

Resources

For Southeastern Wisconsin Residents

Wisconsin Promise
https://promisewi.com/

Autism Society of Southeastern Wisconsin
https://www.assew.org/

Wraparound Milwaukee
http://wraparoundmke.com/

Paragon Community Services
http://www.paragoncommunity.com/

Easter Seals of Southeast Wisconsin
http://www.wi-se,easterseals.com/

Wisconsin Department of Children and Families
https://dcf.wisconsin.gov/

Milwaukee Enrollment Services
https://access.wisconsin.gov/

Independence First
https://www.independencefirst.org/home

Milwaukee Center for Independence
http://www.mcfi.net/MCFI.htm

Respite Care Association of Wisconsin
http://respitecarewi.org/

For United States of America Residents

Parent to Parent USA
http://www.p2pusa.org/p2pusa/sitepages/p2p-home.aspx

Federation for Children with Special Needs
http://fcsn.org/

National Dissemination Center for Children with Disabilities
http://www.parentcenterhub.org/nichcy-gone/

National Collaborative on Workforce and Disability for Youth
http://www.ncwd-youth.info/

Family Voices
http://www.familyvoices.org/

Parents Helping Parents
http://www.php.com/

Goodwill Industries International
http://www.goodwill.org/

Easter Seals
http://www.easterseals.com/

The M.O.R.G.A.N. Project
http://themorganproject.org/

Council for Exceptional Children
http://www.cec.sped.org/

Special Olympics
http://www.specialolympics.org/

The Arc
http://www.thearc.org/

Special Needs Alliance (SNA)
http://www.specialneedsalliance.org/

Sources

1. *Sensory Overloads vs. Behavioral Tantrums: Understanding the Difference and How to Respond* – Children's Therapy Network www.ctn-madison.com
2. *"What's up with Nick?"* – Organization for Autism Research www.researchautism.org
3. *Rain Man DVD* – MGM Home Entertainment
4. *What is Autism*? – Autism Speaks www.autismspeaks.org/what-autism
5. *Autism History* By Dr Ananya Mandal, MD – News Medical Life Science www.news-medical.net/health/Autism-History.aspx

ABOUT THE AUTHOR

Freeman L. Semons, Jr. is the author of three fiction novels *(The Oracle Book, Archangel & The Sixth Commandment)* and the memoir *Uniquely Made*. Besides being a fiction author, Freeman is also an accomplished songwriter/composer, a smooth jazz instrumentalist and a graphic artist/designer. Freeman lives in Wisconsin with his children.

ALSO FROM MORNING BREEZE PUBLICATIONS

Available in Paperback Edition and Kindle Format at Amazon.com

https://www.amazon.com/Archangel-Freeman-L-Semons-Jr/dp/151520586X
https://www.amazon.com/Oracle-Book-Freeman-Semons-Jr/dp/1516883209/

New Smooth Jazz from Morning Breeze Music

MP3 music downloads available at CDBaby.com

https://www.cdbaby.com/cd/freemanlsemonsjr8